AWESOME EMAIL!

10 Email Principles to Improve Your Communication and Accelerate Your Career

By Felix Haller

Copyright © 2020 Felix Haller

All rights reserved. No part of this book may be reproduced or used in any manner without the prior written permission of the copyright owner, except for the use of brief quotations in a book review.

This paperback edition first published in 2020

ISBN: 9798554660917 (Paperback)

Published by Felix Haller
www.felixhaller.org

Your Free Bonus

Thank you for purchasing this book.

I want you to get as much value as possible out of this book and improve your email communication. Therefore, I created a "toolkit" of free bonus materials available for you. You will get:

- **Email principles checklist** and the **AWESOME EMAIL book in PDF** to share with colleagues, friends, and family
- **Free email communication video training** on Udemy
- **Weekly tips** to improve your communication and accelerate your career right into your inbox

Visit www.felixhaller.org/awesome-email to receive the toolkit.

Best,
Felix

Table of Contents

Introduction 1
Why Should You Read This Book? 5
#1 Craft Insightful Subject Lines 11
#2 Think of Your Readers First 19
#3 Clarify Expectations 25
#4 Mention Context, Message, and Actions 33
#5 Write Short Emails 41
#6 Create Scannable Emails 47
#7 Use Bullet Points 53
#8 Simplify Your Writing 59
#9 Leverage Email Functions 63
#10 Reply Promptly and Inline 69
Conclusion 75
Amazon Review 78
Your Free Bonus 79
About the Author 80
Bibliography 81

Introduction

What are the issues with the following email?

Subject: Re: Re: Re: Re: Hey

To: John

Hey,

I know we haven't met, but I believe you work in customer research. I just joined the product development team preparing next week's 2020 customer survey launch to inform our new product roadmap. We have been going back and forth within our team and came up with an initial set of questions. The questions are structured into four categories: demographics, brand perception, product preferences, and suggestions. We are super interested in product preferences since they could tell us if our new potential product will be successful. See attached for the current work-in-progress

AWESOME EMAIL!

version. Cynthia said that you have some survey expertise. I think you were involved in some of the previous customer surveys, right? Were there any interesting learnings or things that surprised you? We think it might be helpful to look at prior surveys. Can someone send us the last couple of surveys? Do you have any other information that you could share with us? Oh, do the questions make sense? Can I call you, or do you want to reply over email? Both are fine. Any thoughts or feedback would be great!

Thanks,
Steven

Issue 1: Useless Subject Line

Steven's subject line is generic and useless. It doesn't give the reader any information about what to expect in the content of the email. The subject line and the sender's name are the most critical factors in determining whether a recipient opens an email.[1] Using a vague and non-descriptive subject line, such as "Hey," "Hi," or "Hello," is

INTRODUCTION

a wasted opportunity to provide useful information to the email recipient.

Issue 2: Long and Unstructured

The email is almost 200 words long. In general, shorter emails are better. Inboxes are flooded with emails, and it takes time and mental energy to read long text. Also, the email lacks structure. It is one long word wall, making it hard to decipher the different messages and questions. The recipient has to read every sentence to understand the key topics and any actions required.

Issue 3: Unclear Purpose

The email lacks a clear goal. Steven talks about the survey questions, previous surveys, general feedback, and scheduling a meeting or call. It is unclear what this email's main purpose is and why Steven is sending it. There are multiple messages and questions all over the place.

AWESOME EMAIL!

Issue 4: Vague Next Steps

Even though Steven mentions a few next steps, they are vague and hidden in a wall of text. Some of his asks are questions, while others are to-dos. For instance, "Can someone send us the last couple of surveys?" is broad and doesn't specify who should work on it and by when. Besides, it is unclear if he expects the reader, John, to reply to his email.

Why Should You Read This book?

Reason 1: Email is everywhere

Email is the most ubiquitous communication tool in the world and impossible to avoid.

An incredible number of emails are sent every day. In 2019 alone, the "Send" button was hit over 300 billion times, resulting in over 100 emails a day per office worker. This number is expected to continue to grow steadily, reaching 350 billion emails sent per day by 2022. Also, more and more people are using email. Global email users added up to 3.9 billion in 2019 and will grow further to around 4.3 billion in 2023. One out of two people globally will be using email.[2]

Even with the emergence of other communication tools, such as chat software and video conferencing, email has remained strong as the primary communication tool in business and isn't going anywhere anytime soon.

If you work in front of a screen, you will spend hours within your email program reading and sending emails every week. On average, office workers spend around 25 percent of their workweek managing emails.[3] That equates to 10 hours in a 40-hour workweek. Said differently, if you were to deal with all of your emails for a given week in a single stretch, you would spend all of Monday and a couple of hours on Tuesday only dealing with emails.

Since email has become the de facto standard for internal communication, most people will write thousands if not millions of emails throughout their careers.

Reason 2: Email communication is critical for your career

Strong communication skills are crucial for your personal and business success, especially since many people are simply not very effective communicators. Their emails are long, unstructured, and cluttered with multiple messages. In contrast, impactful emails

WHY YOU SHOULD READ THIS BOOK?

communicate your message effectively, enable quick responses, and leave a positive impression on you.

Several studies emphasize the importance of communication skills. The largest US business network, LinkedIn, ranked effective communication as the most important soft skill that hiring managers look for in candidates.[4,5] Another study surveying over 300 managers found that effective communication skills are the most desirable quality to consider when hiring college graduates.[6] Unfortunately, communication skills are also seen as the number one incompetency among new hires. Communication is also a critical leadership skill. A Harvard Business Review survey of more than 300,000 professionals ranked being a powerful communicator as one of the top five most important factors impacting a leader's success.[7]

Learning to communicate effectively via email will be of profound effect throughout your career. You might have the best ideas, but they will only catch on if you convey them well.

AWESOME EMAIL!

Reason 3: Practical advice to write effective emails

There are two challenges with email communication in today's business world. First, we get a lot of emails. Second, many are simply not written well, and some are downright bad.

Most of today's email advice focuses on personal productivity, such as the idea of inbox zero, or the technical usage of email programs, such as Microsoft Outlook. This book is not about productivity or any specific tool; it is about improving email communication. I believe that learning what makes a compelling email is what's most important and will significantly improve the quality and reduce the number of emails sent by you and your colleagues.

Over the past six years as a management consultant at Bain & Company, I have sent and received more than ten thousand emails, great ones, okay ones, and bad ones. Luckily, I also had the incredible opportunity to lead high-performing teams, communicate in complex environments, and teach communication skills. Through these experiences, I have learned to appreciate effective email communication.

WHY YOU SHOULD READ THIS BOOK?

As a result, I created this book to share the principles and tactics of effective email communication used by the top management consultants, business leaders, and expert communicators across all businesses. My ultimate goal is for you and everybody else to write clear, concise, and compelling emails. In other words, everybody will get fewer and better emails.

This book is concise and without fluff. You won't find convoluted introductions, all the pros and cons of different tactics, and multiple case studies. Instead, you will learn tactical and practical advice that works.

Reason 4: Immediate results

This book is for everybody who writes emails daily and wants to communicate more effectively.

Do you send emails asking for information? Do you regularly reply to your colleagues' emails? Or do you send multiple emails to your supervisors a day? Then this book is for you! In simpler terms, if you write professional emails, you should read this book.

AWESOME EMAIL!

This book contains practical advice to improve your professional emails. I tailored the principles towards your daily emails, such as updating supervisors or asking colleagues for information.

You can apply all the learnings instantly. Even though each tactic's specificity and impact are different, combining all ten principles will result in your emails being clearer, more concise, and more compelling – in other words, better! You will specifically learn how to do the following:

- Write emails that your colleagues will actually read
- Craft specific and insightful subject lines that provide value to your readers
- Share insights and expectations so that everybody knows how to take action on your emails
- Apply formatting principles to enable your readers to digest your emails quickly
- Respond effectively to avoid miscommunication and confusion

#1 Craft Insightful Subject Lines

Be Specific

The subject line is the first piece of information your recipients will see. People often decide whether to open an email and how much time to spend on it based on the subject line. The subject line is your first opportunity to provide useful information to your recipients. Don't waste it with a useless "Hey" or worse, no subject line at all.

One of the most common problems is vague or one-word subject lines. For example, "Topics," "Question," "Feedback," or "Hey." Those titles don't tell the recipients much. When a recipient receives your email, they should learn what the email is about just by reading your subject line.

Write specific subject lines that tell the audience the message of the email or, even better, what you want the recipients to do. For instance, "Customer meeting changed to tomorrow at 7 p.m.",

AWESOME EMAIL!

"Quick question about your presentation," or "Suggestions for the proposal" are more effective.

Another benefit of being specific is that the more specific you are in the subject line, the less you have to write in the email's body, resulting in concise emails. Specific subject lines also make it easier for your recipients to scan, search, and reference your email. For example, if you write "customer meeting" instead of "customer meeting changed to tomorrow at 7 p.m.," you still need to explain in the body of the email that the meeting time has changed.

You want to explain as much of the email message in the subject line as possible without making it unreadable. Subject lines don't need to be proper sentences; they are more like a few keywords that summarize your email. Using keywords also helps your audience to search and find your email at a later time. Besides, as more and more readers check their email on their phones, a specific subject line will give them the information they need without opening the email.[8]

#1 CRAFT INSIGHTFUL SUBJECT LINES

Example subject lines:

- *"Feedback for your presentation"*
- *"Great customer feedback"*
- *"Initiatives to improve your revenues"*

Appeal to Utility

Effective subject lines indicate usefulness to the recipients. A study at Carnegie Mellon[9] referenced in Daniel H Pink's book *How to Sell*[10] found that recipients are most likely to open and engage with an email if the subject line targets a reader's utility or curiosity.

Email subject lines that focus on utility are most likely to get opened. They directly affect someone's work. For example, the subject line might indicate that the email is a reply to a question they had or is related to their current project.

Curiosity, on the other hand, creates uncertainty. Having some idea of what is in an email but not knowing exactly what to expect can lead to a desire to open an email, but the Carnegie Mellon study

AWESOME EMAIL!

found that curiosity only works well when people aren't busy. When your recipients have a full inbox, they tend to open the more useful emails first.

Since we are getting hundreds of emails a week and are drowning in meetings, appeal to utility in your subject lines to maximize your emails' effectiveness.

Example subject lines:

- *"Answers to your questions about employee engagement"*
- *"Suggestions for your presentation next week"*
- *"Travel details for next week's conference"*

Specify Actions

Often, we send emails to ask someone else to do something, such as sharing a document, providing feedback, or scheduling a meeting. Instead of explaining that ask or action in the email body, convey the full ask in the subject line. Specific and action-oriented subject

#1 CRAFT INSIGHTFUL SUBJECT LINES

lines tell the audience right away what they are expected to do, even without opening the email.

For instance, "Share sales presentation by tomorrow 9 a.m. EST" is a specific and actionable subject line. It clearly states the required action, making reading the email body mostly obsolete and resulting in a shorter, more concise, and more compelling email. On the contrary, "Sales presentation" would be a common but useless subject line.

These "action emails" act as to-dos for the recipient. And since email inboxes serve as to-do lists for many people, your requested task will end up directly on your recipient's "to-do list," increasing the likelihood of them working on and completing it.

Actions should specify what the person needs to do and by when. The more specific you are in terms of the who, what, and when of a to-do, the more likely it is to get completed.

AWESOME EMAIL!

Example subject lines:

- *"Revise August report for reaction by EOD"*
- *"Provide presentation feedback for tomorrow's presentation"*
- *"Schedule a compensation review meeting for us this week"*

Use Prefixes

Subject lines can make the difference between miscommunication and getting things done. Using prefixes or abbreviations in general can further increase the amount of information and meaning you can convey in a subject line.

Prefixes are abbreviations or keywords that allude to what an email is about or what the recipient should do. For instance, writing "FYI" or "for your information" in the subject line tells the recipients that your email does not require any action and is only for informational purposes. Most commonly, prefixes are at the beginning of the subject line, hence the name.

#1 CRAFT INSIGHTFUL SUBJECT LINES

In general, the more information you can communicate in the subject line, the better, and using prefixes in your subject line is another tactic to help with that.

For prefixes to be useful though, the recipients must know what they mean. If you use an abbreviation that your recipient is unfamiliar with, they might get confused. While there are thousands of possible abbreviations listed on Wikipedia[11], limit yourself to a few common and effective ones, such as the following:

- [URGENT] states that your email is urgent and that the reader should read it right away.
- [DRAFT] indicates that the shared email is a draft email and that the sender expects feedback.
- [REQUEST] tells the recipient that the sender is requesting information from the recipient.
- [FYI] communicates to the recipient that the email is only "for your information" and doesn't require a response or action.
- [EOM] means "end of message" and indicates that all the information is in the subject line and nothing in the email body.

AWESOME EMAIL!

Example subject lines:

- *"[URGENT] 10 a.m. meeting canceled"*
- *"[REQUEST] 2019 revenue by division in EUR"*
- *"[FYI] customer survey launched yesterday"*
- *"Call Tom at 303-233-1234 [EOM]"*

#2 Think of Your Readers First

Aim for a "Yes" Response

The only person who matters in email communication is the reader. Great emails provide value to the reader and make it as easy as possible to respond.

Researchers from Carnegie Mellon University found that email recipients are more likely to respond to an email if the email is easy to address, independent of whether the email is important or trivial. On the other hand, important but complex messages require a lot of work to answer and often don't get a response.[12]

Thus, craft emails that only require a short response from your recipients, such as "yes" or "approved." For instance, when asking someone to confirm or acknowledge something, end your email with a "Could you confirm that I can purchase the conference ticket?" or "Do you agree with this approach?" That way, your recipient can

AWESOME EMAIL!

respond "okay," "approved," or "yes" and go deal with their next email.

Too many emails do the opposite, asking several open-ended questions hidden in long paragraphs. We think by providing a lot of detail in our emails, we show the recipients that we are knowledgeable and experts on the topic. Unfortunately, this has the opposite effect. The more questions and longer your email, the less likely it is that the recipient will take any action, and the longer it may take until they respond.[13]

Of course, some emails require more detailed responses from your recipients. Think of your emails on a spectrum of asking only one simple yes or no question to longer emails asking multiple complex questions requiring detailed responses. Move the majority of your emails to the simpler spectrum, asking one simple question. If an email requires the respondents to write a detailed reply, assess whether it is worth it for your readers to spend that much time responding to your email or whether it would be more suitable to discuss it over the phone or in a separate meeting.

#2 THINK OF YOUR READERS FIRST

In summary, distill your email to one ask and design your question so your readers can respond with a simple yes or no.

Double-Check the Recipient's Name

The most important word in every language is our name. We love hearing our names. Dale Carnegie summarized this idea in his best-selling book *How to Win Friends and Influence People*: "a person's name is to that person the sweetest and most important sound in any language."[14] Personalize your email, and especially the greeting line, by including your recipients' names.

Always address your recipients with their correct name, especially making sure you're using the right spelling. This advice sounds straightforward, but the importance can't be overstated. The consequences of misspelling someone's name can be severe. Even though they likely won't call you out for any misspellings, they will notice it and remember it for a long time. In the worst-case scenario, it will damage your reputation and working relationship.

AWESOME EMAIL!

Also, don't shorten somebody's name unless they have asked you to. Don't just assume that calling Michael "Mike" is fine. People are hypersensitive to their names and what they prefer to be called.

Double and triple check your recipients' names. Show your readers that you respect them by addressing them with their correct name. If you are not sure about the correct spelling, look up their name in previous emails, in the signature block, or on LinkedIn.

Personalize and Compliment Your Recipient

Similarity draws people together. Highlighting commonalities or past experiences you have had with the recipient will make your email – and you as a person – more relatable. Mention the last time you met, talk about a hobby you know your recipient likes, or reference some other interesting fact he shared with you.

Also, read up on your recipient's latest publications and successes and compliment them. By showing your recipient that you did your homework and appreciate their work, they will be more willing to respond to your email favorably. That's because this triggers the

#2 THINK OF YOUR READERS FIRST

reciprocity effect, which describes our tendency to reciprocate positive actions, creating a sense of indebtedness.[15]

Be cautious about getting too personal or inserting humor or sarcasm in emails. Humor can get lost in translation without the right tone or facial expression, and what is perceived as funny can be subjective. Several experiments have shown that people significantly overestimate their ability to communicate over email, including misinterpreting humor and sarcasm.[16] It is best to leave out any humor unless you know the recipients well.

#3 Clarify Expectations

Specify the Ask or Action

Whenever you want your email recipients to do something, the most important thing to do to make sure they do it is to be specific on what needs to be done, by whom, and when.

Specifying what you want your readers to complete sounds like a no-brainer. Unfortunately, many emails don't mention what they want the audience to do. An analysis of company emails in a Loughborough University study revealed that only around half of all emails that require recipients to do something stated the specific ask.[17]

Don't be ambiguous about the required action with language such as "Let me know your thoughts." Vague next steps confuse your readers, and when recipients are confused, they tend not to do anything, not even respond. Be extremely clear and specific on what

AWESOME EMAIL!

you want your audience to do. For instance, "Please insert our current pricing structure on page 4 and send the updated version back to me by tomorrow EOD" is specific and clear.

When listing multiple next steps, list them in bullet form and add a section header such as "next steps" or "required actions." A separate section improves visibility, especially for readers who scan your email and look for their to-dos. It's also useful to help your audience with prioritization. If some points are more important than others, state it: "The most important question is X, while Y is optional."

Lastly, if you don't need a response to your email, tell your readers. For example, say "For your information only" or "no action required" to clarify that you don't expect a response or action.

Clarify the Owner

Whenever you need something to be done, you should assign and state the specific owner who should complete the task. Don't assume that someone will proactively complete a request if you don't explicitly mention an owner.

#3 CLARIFY EXPECTATIONS

When someone says, "We should do x" or "It would be nice if we could do y" or "Team – please do z," nobody will do it. If it is not crystal clear to everybody who will own a task, nobody will do it. Ownership and accountability are critical and necessary for effective delegation.

Lastly, adding an "@" before the name is an excellent tactic for assigning owners because it will make it easier for your readers to find the assigned tasks. They can quickly scan your email for their name or use the search functionality in their email software.

Example:

- *"@Sam – Schedule status review meeting for next week."*
- *"Share the final presentation with the team EOW – @Jon."*
- *"Sarah: Please send the final customer survey results to Jon tomorrow to include in the final presentation."*

AWESOME EMAIL!

Share a Deadline

Unless an activity is ongoing, always mention a deadline, even if it is a "fake" deadline. It helps both parties to know when something will be completed and gives the owner an incentive to get it done. It also makes it less intrusive for you to send a follow-up email sometime before or after the deadline has passed.

When setting deadlines or scheduling meetings, specify the exact date and time zone. Asking, "Could you send me the presentation by tomorrow at 9 a.m." might be unclear to your reader. If they are in a different time zone or read the email the next day, they might assume another time or day. In today's business world, with global teams and people working from home, specifying the exact day, time, and time zone by which something is expected will avoid confusion and misunderstandings.

If you know that your recipient works in a different time zone, it is also helpful to do the time zone conversion. For instance, "Would this Friday, 8 a.m. US Eastern Time (8 p.m. Hong Kong Time) work?" Also, if it is critical to specify the date, write out the date in

#3 CLARIFY EXPECTATIONS

full to avoid any confusion, such as "10 September 2020" or "September 10, 2020."

Example:

- *"Schedule our next project status review meeting this week – @Sam."*
- *"@Jon – Share the final presentation with the team by Friday 1 p.m. US Eastern Time."*
- *"@Sarah – Send the final customer survey results to Jon by Thursday 6 p.m. US Pacific Time."*

Suggest Options

You try to schedule a meeting and end your email with "Let me know your availability." Your colleague responds with, "I am quite flexible on Tuesday and Wednesday." Afterward, you go back and forth a couple of times until you finally identify a time slot that works for both of you. That is a common but ineffective approach to scheduling.

AWESOME EMAIL!

Avoid the back-and-forth by always suggesting an exact time and day, even if you don't know the other person's availability. By proposing a time, you put a line in the sand and enable your recipients to make a simple yes-no decision.

If you suggest an exact time, your recipient only needs to check her availability and quickly respond with yes or no. The recommended time will also serve as the default option, resulting in a higher burden on saying no. As a result, your meeting participant will be more inclined to accommodate the time, even if it requires rescheduling other appointments.

Even better, in addition to suggesting a specific time, also share two to three alternatives if the preferred option doesn't work. That way, you increase the chance that your busy colleague can still respond with a simple "yes" to one of your suggested times.

In the best-case scenario, you can see the other person's availability in your organization's calendar application. In that case, look at both of your availabilities and suggest a few times with overlapping availability.

#3 CLARIFY EXPECTATIONS

Example:

- *"Would Tuesday 8–9 a.m. EST work? Alternatively, Wednesday 9–10 a.m. EST?"*
- *"Would one of the following times work?"*
    - *Dec 2, 10–11 a.m. EST (preferred)*
    - *Dec 3, 3–4 p.m. EST*
    - *Dec 4, 8–9 a.m. EST*

#4 Mention Context, Message, and Actions

Clarify Your Email's Purpose

Every email needs a clear purpose. Before writing an email, take a couple of seconds to ask yourself why you are sending this email and whether an email is the best way to achieve your objective. Are you requesting information, providing an update, scheduling a meeting, sharing tasks, or something else?

When your audience opens your email, they want to instantly know your email's purpose and how this email provides value to them. Your readers may access your email in between meetings or in transit. Don't waste their time telling them a long story and making them guess what you want from them. Share your main message within the first 2–3 sentences.

If your objective and message are vague and unclear, your message will fall flat, and you will waste your readers' time, even if the email is well-written. To avoid this, make sure that every email has one clear purpose. Tactically, complete the following sentence for every email, "I am emailing you to inform/ ask/ request/ share ..."

Example:

- *"Tom told me to reach out to you regarding the following information."*
- *"I am emailing you to share the next steps from yesterday's team meeting."*
- *"Our survey results showed that our customers prefer us over our competitors."*

Create a Simple Structure

Effective emails are organized in an easy-to-understand structure, helping readers to quickly grasp the importance and purpose of your email, the highlights of the content, and where immediate action is required.

#4 MENTION CONTEXT, MESSAGE, AND ACTIONS

The structure should always follow the purpose of the email. Ask yourself, what is the most effective format to achieve the email's objective? Is one sentence enough to convince the readers? Should I provide more detail to the recommendations? While structures differ, a popular and practical approach is to have four components in your email: context, message, actions, and details.

Context: Your audience receives hundreds of emails a day, jumps from meeting to meeting, and has to deal with various topics and tasks every day. Every time they open an email, they first want to know why they received the email. Before you bombard them with your message and details, provide context or background information related to your email. Unless your recipient knows the topic well, share your email's context and why they are the right person to respond to your request. For instance, "On Tuesday, we discussed our call center performance," "You sent me an email asking to research young parents' purchasing behavior," or, "Tom suggested reaching out to you since you might have the latest sales forecast."

AWESOME EMAIL!

Message: The message is the purpose and objective of your email. You might want to share the latest customer insights, distribute a PowerPoint presentation, schedule a meeting, or ask your supervisor for feedback. Whatever the message is, it should be specific and concise, optimally no more than 1–2 sentences. If you need more details, separate them from the main message into a few bullets or sentences.

Actions: As described in Chapter 3, actions or next steps represent any activities the readers should do due to your email. Not all emails require direct actions; some are only for informational purposes. Nevertheless, every email should state whether there are any actions required and then specify them.

Details: Even though you want to keep your emails as concise as possible, sometimes you have to provide additional information to support your message or actions. It is good to keep your details to a maximum of 3–4 topics and structure them in bullet form.

#4 MENTION CONTEXT, MESSAGE, AND ACTIONS

Example:

Hi Jon,

In yesterday's status update meeting, we aligned on the near-term next steps related to the product launch. [CONTEXT]

Please find below the aligned next steps [MESSAGE] and prepare to present your updates in next Wednesday's update meeting [ACTIONS]

- *Interview 2–3 key customers to identify product concerns – @Steve [DETAILS]*
- *Update website with refined product descriptions – @Alice [DETAILS]*
- *Create detailed product launch plan – @Jon [DETAILS]*

Best,

Alice

AWESOME EMAIL!

Example:

Hi Jane,

We conducted an extensive customer survey with 1,000 customers. As you requested, I want to share with you the preliminary results for your information. [CONTEXT]

Our customers prefer us over competitors, driven by the product quality and pricing; however, delivery could be improved [MESSAGE]

- 70% NPS score, while competitors have only 20% on average [DETAILS]
- Customers value our product quality and fair pricing [DETAILS]
- Our delivery times are perceived as too slow [DETAILS]

I will present the detailed insights in our meeting on Monday. [ACTIONS]

Best,
Steve

#4 MENTION CONTEXT, MESSAGE, AND ACTIONS

Provide Convincing Details for Your Recommendations

Whenever you share recommendations or insights in an email, you need to convince your readers that your message is correct, which means providing convincing evidence and arguing logically.

A practical approach is called the "pyramid principle."[18] The principle advocates organizing your messages in a logical pyramid structure where every idea synthesizes the ideas and arguments underneath. Each level of the pyramid supports the level above it. The ideas within each level are mutually exclusive and collectively exhaustive.

In practice, this means that your main message is at the top of the pyramid, and your arguments and supporting evidence are below it.

The benefit of the pyramid principle is that it ensures a cohesive argumentation that makes your recommendation stronger. You are telling your audience, "This is my recommendation, and for these three reasons, I believe my recommendation is right." If your audience agrees with the supporting reasons or evidence, the audience logically must agree with your main point.

AWESOME EMAIL!

For instance, in the below example, your recommendation is to sell the new product through Amazon. This is supported by three arguments or pieces of evidence. If the evidence is strong and convincing, your recommendation will be compelling, too.

Tactically, whenever you want to convince your readers of a message, provide supporting insights and evidence organized in a pyramid form.

Example:

We should sell our new product through Amazon [RECOMMENDATION]

- *80% of our customers are digital natives who shop primarily on Amazon [EVIDENCE]*
- *Amazon has shown continuous growth of 15% yearly in our category [EVIDENCE]*
- *Our competitors don't sell on Amazon, giving us a first-mover advantage [EVIDENCE]*

#5 Write Short Emails

Be Concise

Time is precious for you and your audience. Your recipients are busy, and they don't want to spend a lot of time reading your email. They don't need a long story; they want you to get to the point quickly. Thus, the shorter an email, the better.

It is common to write long sentences and paragraphs to explain a message. You struggle to articulate your idea concisely, so you meander. You don't find the right words, so you describe it from multiple angles with different phrases to make sure your recipients get your point. You get off track. All of this results in longer-than-necessary emails that go either unread or unanswered.

Your audience will appreciate shorter emails and respond to them much more quickly.[13] Readers are already struggling with too much information. One in four workers say they feel stressed due to the

AWESOME EMAIL!

volume of information they receive, and half of office workers state that their work's quality suffers because they can't go through all the information available to them.[21] Besides, more than one in three business professionals check their emails on small mobile screens, making concise and brief emails even more critical.[19]

Writing short and concise emails takes time and effort. You need to synthesize your thinking down to the essence and key messages. Emails are not presentations or documents; instead, their purpose is to communicate concisely and only convey what matters. Treat them that way and aim for emails that recipients can read in one or two minutes. If a potential email subject is a complex topic that requires a lengthy discussion, schedule a separate meeting.

Write a Maximum of Five Sentences

At least 90 percent of emails don't need more than five sentences. If you need much more than that, you should probably talk over the phone or discuss the subject in a meeting.

#5 WRITE SHORT EMAILS

Five is not a scientific number, but sticking to a rule of three to five sentences is a highly effective tactic to shorten your emails. Limiting yourself to a few sentences forces you to think concisely, only communicate what is needed, and save time. Also, shorter emails allow your respondents to make quick decisions on what action to take and will increase the likelihood they will reply.

Designer Mike Davidson created a whole philosophy around limiting your emails to a few sentences. Visit his website http://five.sentenc.es/ to add the five-sentence pledge to your signature.[22]

Break up Long Emails

Sometimes we need to convey information in an email that won't fit within a few sentences. In this case, there are two practical approaches: add the detail in an attachment or break your email into separate sections.

Attaching a separate document with the details is the cleanest approach. Attaching documents is especially useful if you already

AWESOME EMAIL!

have your analysis or information readily available in a PowerPoint or Word document. In this case, call out the email's attachment so your recipient knows that additional information is in the attached document. For instance, "I've attached a PowerPoint detailing my initial market research." Also, make sure that you name the file accurately. Don't attach files called "Powerpoint 1". Pick a more insightful name, such as "20200930_Customer Survey results_v01".

Another approach is to separate the email content into sections. For example, create a summary section and a details section. In this case, you explain the email's main points within a few sentences at the beginning of the email. The additional detail will be in a separate section at the bottom of your email, clearly separated from the summary. Create a structure and sections that fit your specific email and tell your audience how the information is structured.

#5 WRITE SHORT EMAILS

Example:

Hi Tom,

Since you asked me to research our customers, I wanted to share with you the key insights from our 2019 customer survey. The detailed findings are at the bottom of this email.

- *Only 30% of customers are satisfied with our products; Company C has 90% satisfaction with its customers*
- *Customers complain about the low quality (80%), high costs (70%), and slow delivery time (50%) of our products*
- *Most customers believe company C has the best products and quality*

Best,

John

DETAILED FINDINGS

[insert here all the additional detail]

#6 Create Scannable Emails

Use White Space, Headlines, and Sections

Attention spans are short, and your recipients are often distracted. They might not read your email word-by-word, especially if you send long and detailed emails. More than nine out of ten US workers confess to deleting or discarding work emails without thoroughly reading them.[21]

Instead, recipients screen incoming messages for relevance and importance and then decide whether to read them. We give emails a rapid review, look for the key insights, and stop reading if we feel the email is lengthy and complicated. We don't like reading a lot of text on a screen, which is tiring for our eyes. Thus, sending an unstructured email with long paragraphs is the easiest way to alienate your readers. Don't do that.

AWESOME EMAIL!

Just as you might with a Word document, use white space, headlines, bullets, and other formatting options to make your emails scannable and the information easy to digest. Headlines and sections are especially useful to help break up large chunks of content and serve as a way to provide orientation to the reader.

Selectively Highlight Important Phrases

Highlighting words or phrases with bolding, underlining, or coloring can improve an email's readability and emphasize key messages.

Selectively bolding a critical point is incredibly impactful to a busy audience scanning your email, especially in long emails. Selective bolding helps your audience to quickly identify and prioritize the most critical insights in your email.

Be mindful and use selective bolding or any other highlighting sparingly. If everything is bold, nothing is bold. An email with too many stylized elements can come across as aggressive or confusing. A good rule of thumb is to identify the two to three points you would

#6 CREATE SCANNABLE EMAILS

want a reader to take away from the email if they only had thirty seconds to read it. Then highlight those points.

Use Standard Fonts and Colors

When thinking about font type and size, the general rule is that your emails should be easy to read. Use standard fonts and formatting, such as Arial, Calibri, or Times New Roman, in a standard size, such as 11- or 12-point font. And obviously, never use a weird-looking font like Comic Sans.

Using black text is the safest choice. Whenever you use any color other than black, there needs to be a reason why. A good reason is to highlight phrases like your key message or your call to action. However, there is usually no good reason to change the standard text; thus, stick with black.

Don't use too many colors and never mix fonts in an email. Yes, your email might be more memorable if you do, but your readers will perceive you as unprofessional.

AWESOME EMAIL!

· · ·

The following example shows how to improve the email from this book's introduction by applying the principles laid out in this chapter without significantly changing the sentences. With the simple addition of white space, sections, and bullets, the reader can quickly scan the email for the key messages and pinpoint where to engage. At the end of the book, we will further improve the email by applying all ten of this book's principles.

Example:

Hey,

I know we haven't met, but I believe you work in customer research? I joined the product development team preparing next week's 2020 customer survey launch to inform our new product roadmap. Cynthia said that you have some survey expertise.

#6 CREATE SCANNABLE EMAILS

We have been going back and forth within our team and came up with a good set of questions.

The questions are structured into four categories: demographics, brand perception, product preferences, and suggestions.

We are super interested in the product preferences since they could tell us if our new potential product will be successful.

- *I think you were involved in some of the previous customer surveys, right? Were there any interesting learnings or things that surprised you?*
- *We think it might be helpful to look at previous surveys. Can someone send us the last couple of surveys?*
- *Do the questions make sense?*
- *Do you have any other information that could help us?*

Can I call you, or do you want to reply over email? Both are fine. Any thoughts or feedback would be great!

Thanks,
Steve

#7 Use Bullet Points

Replace Paragraphs with Bullet Points

Long paragraphs in emails are ineffective. The problem with long forms of text is that they are strenuous to read and make it challenging to identify key messages.

Therefore, whenever possible, replace paragraphs with bullet points, especially when communicating lists, whether it be a list of questions, insights, actions, or agenda items.

Bullet points add structure, organization, and white space to your emails, all of which result in improved readability and a visual and organizational break between your main ideas. The bullet points clarify where one point ends, and another one begins. All of this is way harder in paragraph form.

In addition, bullet points force the sender to be concise. In general, shorter bits of information are better since they are easier to read and

AWESOME EMAIL!

digest. You can shorten a fifty-word section to merely a fraction of that by synthesizing the key themes into a few bullet points. Forcing yourself to use bullet points will save you and your readers time.

Numbering a list of bullets further improves the structure and makes it easier to reference a specific bullet point. When your supervisor comments on question number seven, you can be sure you are both talking about the same issue.

> **Weak example:**
>
> *In yesterday's meeting, we aligned on a few next steps. Jamie, you mentioned you would update the business case with the latest pricing forecasts, right? We should also draft the press release for product A and talk to 50+ priority customers to identify product consideration. Jack, you should do both of them.*

#7 USE BULLET POINTS

Good example:

We aligned on the following next steps:

- *Update the business case with the latest pricing forecasts – @Jamie*
- *Draft the press release for product A – @Jack*
- *Talk to 50+ priority customers to identify product considerations – @Jack*

Apply the Rule of Three

The rule of three is a classic writing principle and has been used and applied over centuries. Caesar said, "Veni, Vedi, Vici"; the bible states, "Father, Son, and Holy Spirit," and the US constitution reads "Life, Liberty and the pursuit of Happiness."

The principle states that ideas and lists of three things are more effective and memorable than other numbers. A list of three things is the right mix of brevity and rhythm, creating a pattern that makes it easier to remember. It is simple and catchy. Academics have studied the impact of threes for centuries and concluded that we are hardwired to respond positively to groups of three.

AWESOME EMAIL!

Thus, to make your lists more impactful, synthesize them into three items if possible, but don't force it. As a rule of thumb, groups of three to five are most effective, and the longer the list, the more likely your audience won't remember any of them.

For instance, if you want to inform your supervisor about the sales organization's issues, you might create the following long list.

- *Sales reps complain about their below-market pay.*
- *Our direct competitors pay their sales reps more*
- *Our sales reps are less productive than competitors*
- *Sales rep turnover is high*
- *Sales reps are dissatisfied with the cumbersome CRM user interface*
- *Our new CRM system requires extensive training*

Even though this list is more effective than a long paragraph, a more impactful email would synthesize them further into three to five key insights instead of all six. Your reader will likely care about the key issues and not every possible one. Applying the rule of three to the previous bullet points could lead to the following concise three bullet points:

#7 USE BULLET POINTS

- *Our sales reps are dissatisfied with their pay*
- *Our sales reps are less productive than competitors*
- *The CRM system user interface is cumbersome*

Utilize Parallelism

Using parallel structure in your emails and bullets points adds both impact and clarity to your writing. It increases the readability of your writing and makes your text and messages easier to understand.

Parallelism is the repetition of a chosen grammatical form within a sentence. By making each item or idea in a group follow the same grammatical pattern, you create parallel construction.

Let's look at an example of initiatives written in a non-parallel structure. Even the casual reader will notice that they do not feel consistent and professional, and it is harder to understand how the ideas fit together.

AWESOME EMAIL!

- *Increasing revenues by developing a new product*
- *To reorganize the sales organization will increase flexibility*
- *We will reduce purchasing costs through vendor consolidation*

Compare the previous example with the same initiatives written in a parallel structure. All three sentences are in an active voice, start with the same verb structure (i.e., "develop," "reorganize," and "consolidate"), and are followed by the expected result in the same format (i.e. "to increase," "to improve," and "to reduce").

- *Develop a new product to increase revenues*
- *Reorganize our sales organization to improve flexibility*
- *Consolidate vendors to reduce purchasing costs*

#8 Simplify Your Writing

Write Proper and Simple Sentences

Emails are different from texts or chats, where it is more accepted to write casually or informally. When writing emails, you want to come across as professional, trusted, and credible. Thus, your emails must be written in proper English grammar, using sentence case and capitalizing the first letter in a sentence.

Also, simple language is more comfortable for your audience to digest and ultimately leads to higher response rates. Boomerang, an email productivity company, found that emails written at a third-grade reading level received the highest response rates. Those emails received almost 40 percent higher response rates than emails written at a college reading level and nearly 20 percent higher rates than emails written at a high-school reading level.[24]

AWESOME EMAIL!

Avoid lengthy and complicated sentences and, instead, break long sentences into short ones and use easy-to-understand words. By doing so, you are subtly telling your reader that you respected them enough to put in the time to make your writing easy to follow.

Before sending any email, read it over and take out any extraneous wording and unnecessary information. Using an online readability test (www.online-utility.org) is a good starting point to check your emails.

Use Active Voice

Powerful writing is direct and forceful. Be decisive by using the active voice. William Strunk Jr. described the active voice in his monumental "Elements of Style" as "more direct and vigorous than the passive," and said that it "makes for forcible writing."[25]

Using active voice encourages action and responsibility and makes your sentences easier to read. In active-voice sentences, the subject does the activity. In passive voice, the subject does nothing; it merely receives the action. For instance, "John hired a new sales

#8 SIMPLIFY YOUR WRITING

director" is written in the active voice, while "A new sales director was hired" is passive.

That doesn't mean there isn't a place for the passive form in emails. The passive can be appropriate to avoid pointing fingers and allow for ambiguity and nuance. For instance, instead of "You did it wrong," saying, "It seems like the instructions weren't followed properly" is better if it is unclear who did something or you don't want to call somebody out.

Remove Unnecessary Words and Phrases

Vigorous writing is concise and clear. Therefore, avoid any words that don't add meaning but make your emails unnecessary long and slow down the reader. Also, avoid unclear and ambiguous wording, which makes your emails less convincing.

For instance, replace the word "very." There is almost always a more apt word choice available than "very," so using it shows your readers that you didn't put in the required time to improve your

AWESOME EMAIL!

writing. Look for "very" in your emails and replace it with another more descriptive and specific word.

An excellent example of a word that makes your message appear timid and lacks conviction is "just." Instead of "I just want to request more information" or "I just wanted to tell you," say, "I want to request more information" or "I want to tell you." Scrapping the "just" makes your emails more assertive and straightforward.

Other words to reduce are "basically," "actually," "really," "obviously," and "honestly," among others.

Example:

- "Very important" can be replaced with "critical."
- "Very often" can be replaced with "frequently."
- "I just want to ..." can be replaced with "I want to ..."

#9 Leverage Email Functions

Use a Signature

A signature is a personalized block of text at the end of an email that contains the sender's contact information. Adding a signature to your emails shows professionalism and helps your readers quickly find your detailed contact information.

A signature should be simple and subtle. Only include your name, position, phone number, company website, and potentially your LinkedIn URL. Don't clutter it with quotes, pictures, etc. If your company has a standard format for email signatures, stick with it.

And don't add a "Sent from my phone" note or any other message that implies that the email might not be up to standard because you quickly typed it on your phone. There is no excuse for poorly-

AWESOME EMAIL!

written emails with typos unless you don't care if your recipients think you are unprofessional and potentially lazy.

Be Purposeful with Email Fields

When sending an email, the sender has three options on how to send the mail: "To," "CC," or "BCC." Each of them has a different purpose and should be used precisely for their intended purpose.

The To field should only contain the recipients that must see the email. That usually means the recipients you expect to respond to your email (unless your email is solely for informational purposes).

Using CC (carbon copy) appropriately can be powerful. The purpose of CC is to provide visibility for someone, such as your supervisor. It is like saying, "Read the email but don't feel obligated to reply." In rare instances, using the CC field to include someone with clout can pressure the recipient to respond. For example, if you ask someone to provide you information or to respond and you CC their boss or the CEO, they will likely respond quickly. Use this tactic

#9 LEVERAGE EMAIL FUNCTIONS

selectively and optimally get approval from the senior person you are CC-ing.

Knowing the purpose of email fields is only half the battle. We tend to add too many addresses in the To and CC fields of our emails. A study of company emails showed that almost one in five emails had unnecessary people CC-ed other than the primary recipients.[17] The problem with adding too many email addresses is that the more people you send an email to, the less likely anybody will respond to it, and the shorter the responses you do receive will be. This effect, which is called the diffusion of responsibility or bystander effect, has been intensely studied.[23] Thus, ask yourself, "Who needs to see and respond to this email?" Delete everybody else.

Lastly, to prevent accidentally sending an unfinished draft email, leave the email fields blank until your email is proofread and final. I always write the email first, refine it, and then last, enter the email addresses in the correct To and CC fields.

AWESOME EMAIL!

Don't Use BCC

BCC, or blind carbon copy, sends an email to someone without anybody else seeing their name. For example, if you send an email to your colleague Alex and BCC your supervisor Jack, Alex won't know that your supervisor also received the email.

In business, avoid BCC. Transparency is essential, and sending someone an email and secretively including someone else is dishonest and can impact your credibility and reputation. There are a couple of instances where using BCC makes sense.

First, BCC can be appropriate when emailing a large group of people to protect their email addresses. For example, if you share an upcoming meeting or webinar with many customers, you don't want the customers to see each other's email addresses. Putting them all in BCC allows you to send one mass email to all of them without the customers seeing each other.

In contrast, though, if you want someone to see a message for information purposes without telling the other recipients, send the email to the To and CC recipients and then forward the original

#9 LEVERAGE EMAIL FUNCTIONS

email. Forwarding an email avoids the BCC recipient unintentionally hitting reply all and exposing that they were secretly on BCC. Sometimes people get emails and don't even check whether the sender put them as To, CC, or BCC. Forwarding an email avoids that. They won't be able to reply to the original recipients.

The second instance in which using BCC makes sense is moving people to BCC to remove them from an ongoing email thread. This is a good practice. For example, if your supervisor introduces you to someone else, it is good practice to move your supervisor to BCC and comment, "moving Alex to BCC." That way, your supervisor has visibility that you own the relationship going forward without getting flooded with endless emails.

Use Out-of-Office Replies

Out-of-office (OOO) replies are auto-response emails that get automatically sent when someone emails you. Auto-responses are practical if you know you won't be able to respond within a reasonable amount of time, for instance, being on vacation or at a

AWESOME EMAIL!

conference for a few days. Only create OOO replies if you know you won't be able to respond for a significant period of time. If you are only out of the office for a day, there is no need to set up an OOO reply.

Good OOO replies tell recipients why you are not available, specify the exact time you will be back, and mention a point of contact for urgent requests. You are thereby providing transparency to colleagues trying to reach you and managing expectations when you will get back to them. Inserting "OOO" or "Out of Office" in the subject line is good practice, so your recipients can immediately identify your response as an out-of-office reply instead of a personally-written email.

For example, "I am on vacation until December 5th, 2020, and won't get back to you before then. Please reach out to John at john@company.com for urgent requests."

#10 Reply Promptly and Inline

Respond Promptly to Time-Sensitive Emails

Even though you don't have to reply to all emails, a reply or acknowledgment serves as good email etiquette, especially if you work in the same organization as the sender.

More importantly, though, try to reply immediately to time-sensitive emails. Even if you can't solve the request right away, it is good practice to acknowledge that you received the message and share what you will do next. Your response will calm the sender and manage expectations. The problem with not replying is that the sender doesn't know how to interpret silence. Is the recipient already working on the ask? Is she out for lunch? Or should I call her to explain the situation?

Apart from responding promptly to urgent messages, the appropriate response time depends on the sender and email type. For emails from colleagues within your organization, respond within twenty-four hours. For your immediate team, a same-day response is recommended. Your team expects you to check your emails a couple of times a day, and most of your team's requests will be timely matters. You don't need to solve the full question in your reply, but similar to time-sensitive emails, acknowledging that you have read the email and sharing what you will do next is worthwhile.

The appropriate response time for emails from outside the organization is more ambiguous. Unless the email is urgent, responding at the end of the week is typically appropriate. For high-value contacts, it is best to respond quicker, within twenty-four hours.

Reply to Questions Inline

When replying to questions in an email, replying inline makes your communication clearer and more legible. Inline replies are responses in the original email body right after the question instead of answers at the top in a new email. Alternatively, you can also

#10 REPLY PROMPTLY AND INLINE

copy and paste the sender's asks in a new email and then respond to the requests one by one.

When responding, make sure other respondents can quickly identify your responses and tell them apart from other responses. Use a different color, bold your answer, or otherwise state that you added the inline response. Also, respond immediately after the question or after the last reply. Lastly, if the questions aren't visually separated, separate them yourself in a new email and then respond inline after each question.

There are a few benefits of inline responses. First, inline replies ensure that you respond to all questions. For instance, if someone asks a few questions in an email chain and someone else asks additional questions, you need to scroll through a couple of emails and answer them separately. If everybody replies in the original email's body, all the questions and responses will be consolidated in one section, leading to shorter email chains and better organization

Second, with inline responses, it is easier to decipher who said what and when. If each respondent uses a different color and answers below the last response, it is clear who said what. The approach is similar to replies on a social media post. The comments are ordered chronologically, and each answer can be attributed to one person.

Make Sure Your Response Is Meaningful

Every time you respond, you send another email to someone's inbox. You are asking your respondents to look at your email and decide what it means for them. As a result, you create work for someone else, even if your email is just for informational purposes or only takes a few minutes to read. The minutes add up, particularly if you send your email to multiple recipients several times a week.

Thus, before you reply to an email, make sure your response is necessary or meaningful. The two critical questions to ask are: "Does the sender expect me to respond?" and "Is my response adding value to the recipients?"

First, the most obvious response is to a specific question or ask stated in the email. If the sender expects you to respond, you should obviously respond. As discussed in Chapter 3, write specific actions in your emails, detailing what you expect your audience to do. Also,

#10 REPLY PROMPTLY AND INLINE

specify when you don't expect your audience to respond by saying, "Feel free to archive," "No response or action required," or "For your information."

Second, responses have to be meaningful. A simple "okay" reply is not meaningful unless it is essential to acknowledge that you have read the email and the sender expects your response. It's better to reply with additional information and thoughts that add value to the conversation.

Don't Reply All

In theory, reply all is a useful email feature, but it can be horrible if misused. Reply all is great if you are part of an email chain with only a few colleagues, and you want everybody to have visibility and comment.

But the downside of hitting reply all is that the email will likely be irrelevant for many recipients. Since everybody gets the email in their inbox, they need to pay attention to it. Every time someone hits reply all, every recipient gets another email – and ignoring emails

AWESOME EMAIL!

can be almost impossible, with instant email notifications and the habit of checking our inboxes several times a day.

Thus, only reply all if you are confident that the response should go to all the recipients on the original email, and you need them to respond. Don't use reply all if the email only needs to go to the sender or a subset of the email recipients. For example, quick acknowledgment emails, such as a "Thanks!" or "Agree," don't need to go to everybody.

Like the BCC functionality, mention when you make changes to the recipients on an email chain, especially when you remove someone. A simple "I am removing Mike and Sarah from the email" is good practice.

Conclusion

This book started with an example of a common but ineffective email. The email had a useless subject line, was too long and unstructured, had a vague purpose, and did not contain specific and clear next steps.

Leveraging this book's email principles, the sender could significantly improve his email. In the below example, I applied the most critical principles, such as crafting a useful subject line, formatting the email, using bullet points, and writing clear next steps to improve Steven's email.

Example:

Subject: Support 2020 customer survey

Hey John,

AWESOME EMAIL!

The product development team is preparing next week's 2020 customer survey launch, which will inform our new product roadmap.

Cynthia told me to reach out to you due to your extensive market research experience.

Could you help us provide the following three pieces of information by Friday, EOD? Please quickly confirm whether that timeline is realistic and whether I should reach out to somebody else.

<u>Next steps</u>

- *Share the 2019 customer survey questions and insights – @John*
- *Provide feedback on the attached preliminary survey questions – @John*
- *Share additional insights that could inform the customer survey – @Johnt*

Thanks,

Steven

CONCLUSION

It is evident that the updated email is clearer, more concise, and more compelling than the unedited version. The reader can quickly identify the context and purpose of the email: "Support 2020 customer survey" and "Provide three pieces of information by Friday." Besides, the next steps section is visually separated from the rest of the email, and the bullet points make it easy to digest the next steps.

By reading this book, I hope you have learned and internalized the email principles and tactics and are ready to embark on your journey to improve your email communication. While some of the principles will help you get better instantly, some might take longer to stick. By applying the 10 email principles, you will improve your email communication and accelerate your career.

Amazon Review

Thanks for reading this book.

If you enjoyed this book, I'd be super grateful if you could leave an honest review of it on Amazon. It'll only take one minute of your time, but it will mean the world to me because every single review counts.

Visit www.felixhaller.org/email-review or Amazon.com to leave a review

Also, I poured my heart into this book and would love to hear your feedback and questions. If you have any thoughts, please don't hesitate to contact me at www.felixhaller.org or **(404) 666-9949.**

Thanks so much for your kind support!

Best,

Felix

Your Free Bonus

As mentioned in the beginning of the book, I created a free "toolkit" of free bonus materials available for you. You will get:

- **Email principles checklist** and the **AWESOME EMAIL book in PDF** to share with colleagues, friends, and family
- **Email communication video training** on Udemy
- **Weekly tips** to improve your communication and accelerate your career right into your inbox

Visit www.felixhaller.org/awesome-email to receive the toolkit.

Best,
Felix

About the Author

Felix Haller is a lifelong learner, optimist, and business enthusiast.

He worked as a management consultant at the global management consulting company Bain & Company for almost six years. As a manager, he led and coached project teams in various industries and capabilities, including strategy, mergers and acquisitions, and performance improvement.

Over the last decade, he has lived, worked, and studied in China, Germany, the Netherlands, and the US. He holds degrees from the Rotterdam School of Management (The Netherlands), Fudan University (China), and the Ludwig Maximilian University (Germany).

He lives in Atlanta with his wife Shannon and pup Picasso.

For more information, visit www.felixhaller.org.

Bibliography

1. SuperOffice. Email Open Rates: A Scientific, Step by Step Guide for 2020. https://www.superoffice.com/blog/email-open-rates/.

2. Daily number of emails worldwide 2023. https://www.statista.com/statistics/456500/daily-number-of-e-mails-worldwide/.

3. Chui, M. et al. The social economy: Unlocking value and productivity through social technologies. https://www.mckinsey.com (2015).

4. Barnes, B. What You Need to Know to Get Hired This Month: August 2020. https://blog.linkedin.com/2020/august/17/what-you-need-to-know-to-get-hired-this-month-august-2020.

5. Berger, G. Data Reveals The Most In-Demand Soft Skills Among Candidates. https://business.linkedin.com/talent-solutions/blog/trends-and-research/2016/most-indemand-soft-skills.

6. Weldy, T. G. & Icenogle, M. L. A Managerial Perspective: Oral Communication Competency Is Most Important for Business Students in the Workplace Jeanne D. Maes. Journal of Business Communication vol. 34 67–80 (1997).

7. The Skills Leaders Need at Every Level. https://hbr.org/2014/07/the-skills-leaders-need-at-every-level (2014).

8. Mobile Email Statistics. https://99firms.com/blog/mobile-email-statistics.

9. Wainer, J., Dabbish, L. & Kraut, R. Should I open this email? Proceedings of the 2011 annual conference on Human factors in computing systems – CHI '11 (2011) DOI:10.1145/1978942.1979456.

10. Pink, D. H. To Sell Is Human: The Surprising Truth About Moving Others. (Penguin, 2012).

11. Contributors to Wikimedia projects. List of email subject abbreviations. https://en.wikipedia.org/wiki/List_of_email_subject_abbreviations (2010).

12. Dabbish, L. A., Kraut, R. E., Fussell, S. & Kiesler, S.

Understanding email use. Proceedings of the SIGCHI conference on Human factors in computing systems – CHI '05 (2005) DOI:10.1145/1054972.1055068.

13. Kooti, F., Aiello, L. M., Grbovic, M., Lerman, K. & Mantrach, A. Evolution of Conversations in the Age of Email Overload. Proceedings of the 24th International Conference on World Wide Web – WWW '15 (2015) DOI:10.1145/2736277.2741130.

14. Carnegie, D. & General Press. How to Win Friends and Influence People. (GENERAL PRESS, 2016).

15. Hollingworth, C. Bias in the spotlight: reciprocity. http://www.research-live.com/article/opinion/bias-in-the-spotlight-reciprocity/id/4013678.

16. Kruger, J., Epley, N., Parker, J. & Ng, Z.-W. Egocentrism over email: can we communicate as well as we think? J. Pers. Soc. Psychol. 89, 925–936 (2005).

17. How much does email cost a business? https://www.sciencedaily.com/releases/2011/05/110509100940.htm.

18. Minto, B. The Pyramid Principle: Logic in Writing and

Thinking. (Pearson Education, 2009).

19. Forsey, C. The Ultimate List of Email Marketing Stats for 2020. https://blog.hubspot.com/marketing/email-marketing-stats.

20. McDermott, A. Information Overload Is Crushing You. Here are 11 Secrets That Will Help. https://www.workzone.com/blog/information-overload/ (2017).

21. New Survey Reveals Extent, Impact of Information Overload on Workers; From Boston to Beijing, Professionals Feel Overwhelmed, Demoralized. https://www.lexisnexis.com/community/pressroom/b/news/posts/new-survey-reveals-extent-impact-of-information-overload-on-workers-from-boston-to-beijing-professionals-feel-overwhelmed-demoralized.

22. Sentenc.es – A Disciplined Way To Deal With Email. https://sentenc.es/.

23. Barron, G. & Yechiam, E. Private email requests and the diffusion of responsibility. Computers in Human Behavior vol. 18 507–520 (2002).

24. Moore, A. 7 Tips for Getting More Responses to Your Emails (With Data!). https://blog.boomerangapp.com/2016/02/7-tips-for-getting-more-responses-to-your-emails-with-data/ (2016).

25. Strunk, W. The Elements of Style: The Original Edition. (Courier Corporation, 2012).

www.ingramcontent.com/pod-product-compliance
Lightning Source LLC
Chambersburg PA
CBHW070437220526
45466CB00004B/1717